KESLER WOODWARD
North and South

ESSAY BY FRANK SOOS

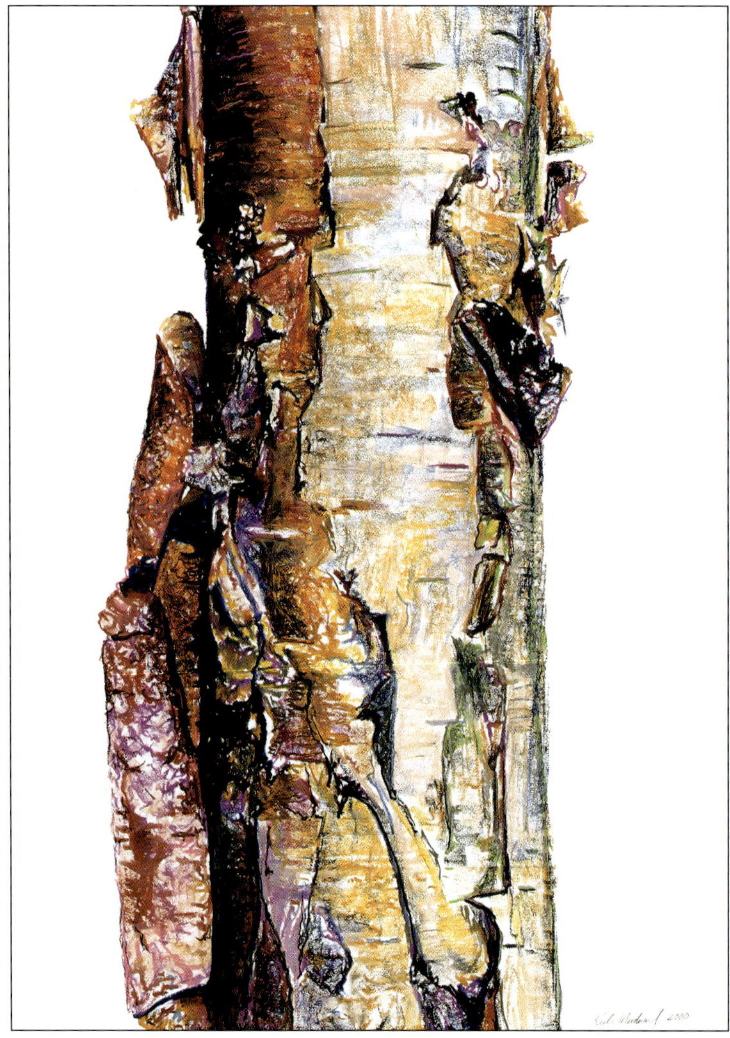

Bright Birch #1, 2000
oil pastel on paper
42 x 30 inches

Published in conjunction with an exhibition organized by the Morris Museum of Art in cooperation with the Jerald Melberg Gallery. Exhibition dates: January 11 - April 8, 2001, Morris Museum of Art, Augusta, Georgia, and April 12 - May 19, 2001, Jerald Melberg Gallery, Charlotte, North Carolina.

© 2001 Morris Museum of Art, 1 Tenth Street, Augusta, Georgia 30901. All rights reserved.

Photography by David Ramsey, Charlotte, North Carolina.
All works of art courtesy of Jerald Melberg Gallery, Charlotte, North Carolina.
Design: Vince Bertucci, Morris Communications Corporation.

In Frank Soos' essay, the quote from Donald Barthelme is taken from "Not Knowing,"
reprinted in *Best American Essays of 1986*, Robert Atwan and Elizabeth Hardwick,
eds., New York: Ticknor & Fields, 1986. Annie Dillard's quote is taken from
An American Childhood, New York: Harper & Row, 1987.

Cover image: Kesler Woodward, **Appalachian Spring** (detail)

ISBN: 1-890021-13-X

Foreword

With the opening of the exhibition *Kesler Woodward, North and South,* the Morris Museum of Art presents a selection of recent paintings by an artist who was born in the South but has lived and worked as an artist in Alaska for more than twenty-five years. We first encountered Kes Woodward's work in 1995 when one of his paintings was acquired for the art collection at the *Juneau Empire,* a newspaper owned by Morris Communications Corporation. That event has led to a series of collaborations that link our common interests in Alaska and the Southeastern United States, and we have come to know Kes as an artist, an art historian, a curator, a teacher, and a friend.

Over the past few years, as business has taken us from Augusta to Alaska, my wife, Sissie, and I have been able to spend time with Kes and his family, and we have come to appreciate the connections he has to the land and the places where he feels at home. We also have come to know his dedication to art—his personal expression of those complex connections. He is an articulate ambassador for the art and artists of Alaska, and with this exhibition, he explores territory at once old and familiar, and new and challenging: the land where he grew up, before he settled far away.

It is Kes Woodward's approach to this new challenge that writer Frank Soos explores eloquently in his essay. And it is Kes's enthusiastic response to the challenge that the Morris Museum of Art presents in this exhibition of works from both the Far North and the Southeast. As these paintings clearly show, Kes Woodward is at home on both sides of the continent.

William S. Morris III
Chairman of the Board of Trustees
Morris Museum of Art

Acknowledgments

Two core aspects of my identity, Southern-ness and Northern-ness, have been for much of my life like twin ships, sailing at opposite corners of the continent on courses seemingly fated never to cross. I was born and grew up on a cotton farm within a few miles of the land on which my family settled in South Carolina in the eighteenth century. I went to college in North Carolina and married a Virginia woman. My Southern roots are very deep. But I have spent almost my entire adult life in Alaska, forging a career as a Northern artist, curator, and art historian. The Far North has become as much my home, and as much a part of my self-image, as the South that is in my genes.

In recent years, against all expectation, the Morris Museum of Art has made it possible for those two ships to come within hailing distance of each other. I was honored to be asked to speak at the opening of an exhibition of Alaskan art at the Morris Museum in 1997. In 1998 I spoke again in Augusta, at the opening of a retrospective exhibition which I organized for the Morris Museum and the Anchorage Museum of History and Art on the work of Eustace Ziegler, one of Alaska's most beloved historical painters.

In the current exhibition of my own work, I have been afforded the opportunity to explore those two geographic poles of my identity. Despite their cultural differences, Southerners and Alaskans seem similarly, peculiarly, bonded to the land. I must have received a double dose of attachment to place. Each image here is of a particular place important to me. South Boundary Boulevard in Aiken, South Carolina—still perhaps the most beautiful street I have seen in the world. The apple farm my wife Missy grew up on in Virginia—land on which I have spent much time and which I have come to know and love as if it had been my own home. The endless Northern forests and mighty mountain ranges of interior Alaska, where I have lived, hiked, hunted, and painted for the last quarter century and many places in between.

I have a number of people to thank for this extraordinary opportunity. I am grateful for the friendship and support of William Morris III, Chairman of the Board of Trustees of the Morris Museum of Art, whose delight in both the Deep South and the Far North is equal to my own. It is his vision of building bridges between these disparate regional cultures that has created an institution and a climate in which such an exhibition as this could originate.

Louise Keith Claussen, Director of the Morris Museum, is the kind of museum director every curator and every artist hopes to work with one day. I feel very fortunate to have had the opportunity to work with her on several projects in the last half-dozen years. Combining my

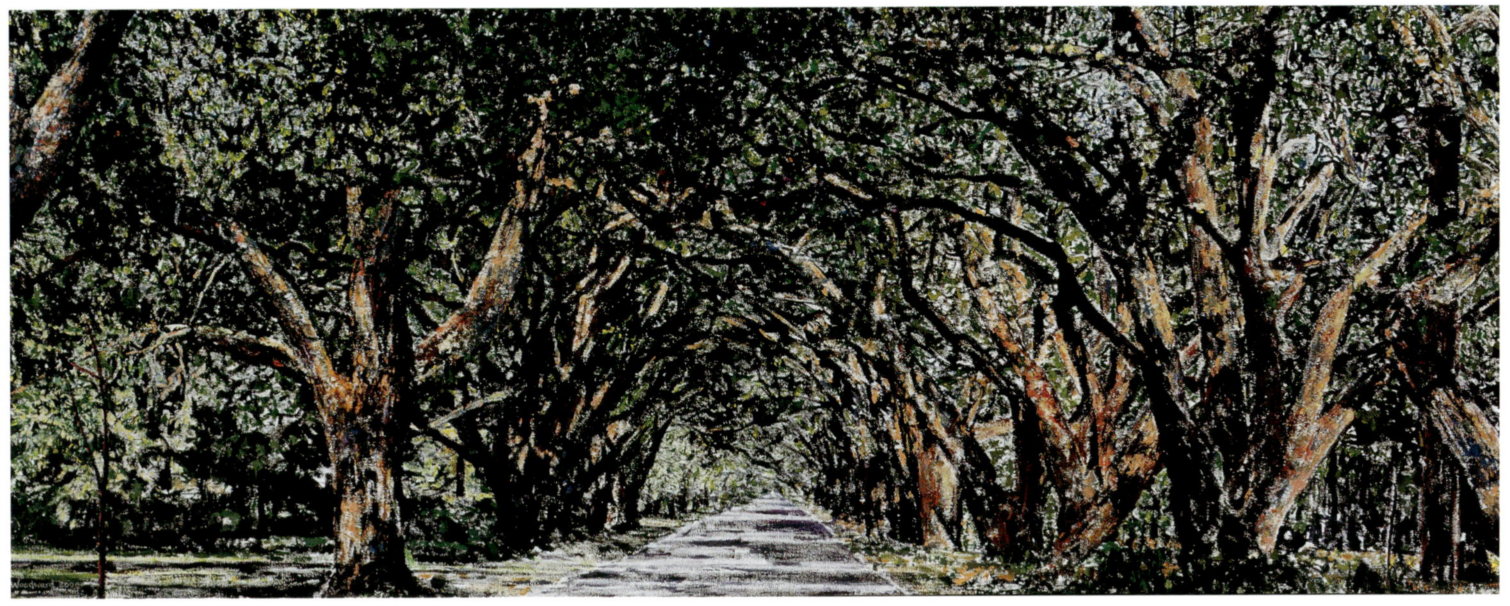

SOUTH BOUNDARY, 2000
oil on canvas
23¹/₂ x 59¹/₂ inches

Southern and Northern imagery in a single showing was her inspiration, and it is to her that I owe thanks for both the invitation to undertake this exhibition and the enthusiasm and ability to bring it to fruition.

Jerald Melberg Gallery in Charlotte, North Carolina, has been the primary representative of my work throughout the country for more than a decade and a half. Jerald's unflagging energy, enthusiasm, and support have enabled me to live in a remote corner of the North American continent and still have my work seen and placed in collections throughout the country. His and his staff's willingness and capability to undertake every aspect of preparation of the work for this exhibition, from building stretchers and stretching the canvases to photographing the work for the catalogue, made this show possible.

I am likewise privileged to have a writer of the quality of Frank Soos write the catalogue essay for the exhibition. Frank, Missy, and I attended Davidson College together, and by chance he came to teach at the University of Alaska a few years after our arrival. A widely recognized author, recipient of a National Endowment for the Arts Fellowship, and recent winner of the Flannery O'Connor Award for Short Fiction, he brings to the examination of my work great gifts as a writer. But he also brings to it years of fishing and walking in the woods with me, looking at my paintings, discussing ideas about art and writing, and sharing a similar range of experience with both the South and the North.

No acknowledgment on my part could be complete without my deepest thanks to Herb Jackson, my undergraduate painting teacher, who not only taught me most of what I know about making paintings, but also convinced me by inspiration and example that making art was a high calling. And finally, to Missy, my wife of thirty years, who took me to my first art museum, lured me to my first art class, and who remains my most cherished and essential support.

Kesler Woodward
Fairbanks, Alaska
October 2000

THEODORE'S PLACE, 2000
oil crayon on paper
12 ¾ x 39 ½ inches

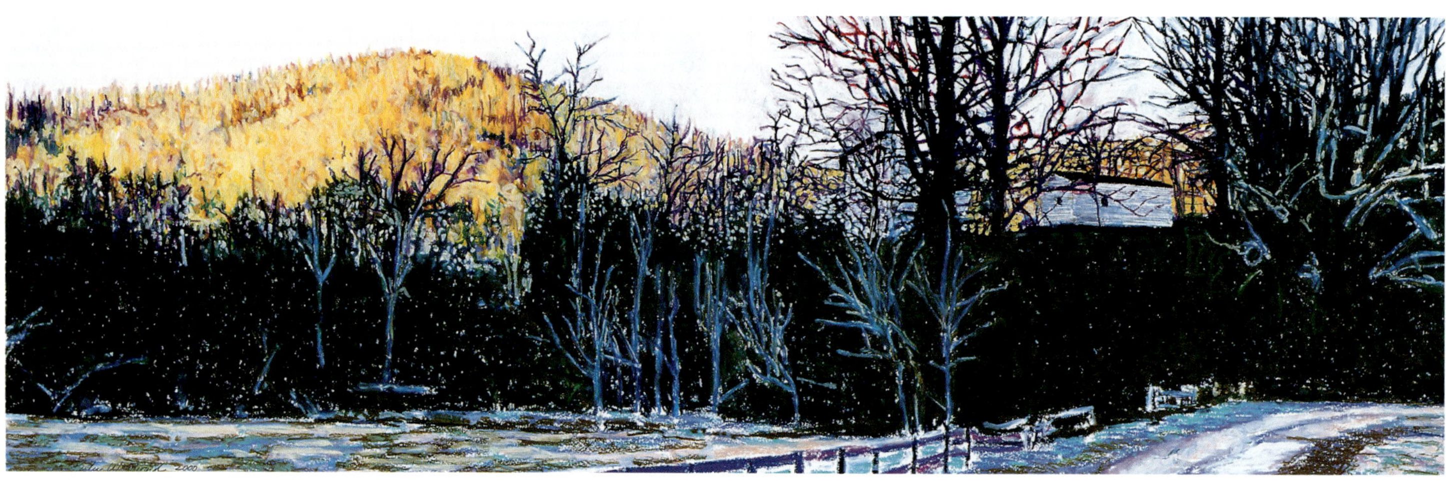

Entering the Landscape

Kes Woodward's Paintings of North and South

BY FRANK SOOS

Thirty years ago, when Kes Woodward was studying painting at Davidson College in North Carolina, I doubt he gave much thought to landscape. A visiting painter assured him that all there was left of landscape could be viewed from a car window: a regularly mowed median strip moving along at sixty-five miles an hour. Nobody thought to disagree with him. The Davidson campus was home to some mighty big oaks, tended and trussed up and nursed through their every ailment and grievous amputation. There was nothing of what you'd call an understory at all, just a carefully maintained lawn and little thumbnail plots of perennials we hardly noticed as we hurried to and from classes. Such touches were for our parents. Maybe the visiting artist got it right. The natural world in the small-town, still pre-suburban South had been pushed back to flower beds in front of public buildings and banks, and one of those honored old oaks on every village green.

Kes Woodward was stretching canvases on old screen doors and experimenting with color and shape, experiments that involved masking tape and a garden hose. In those heady days, that's mostly what people were thinking about in the painting world, color and shape. The experiments were and still are well worth the effort.

Ten years later, Kes had fetched up in Fairbanks, Alaska, nearly as far to the North and West as his intentional drifting could carry him. What is it about this place, Alaska? Keep in mind that it's a mighty big place and that Kes made extended stops in Juneau and Anchorage before he finally came to rest in Fairbanks. In those other places, the geography is more insistent. Juneau's mountains and glaciers tumble right out into Gastineau Channel; the town clings precariously to the hillsides as if it might just slide into the sea as well. In Anchorage, the Chugach Mountains backlight the city, sometimes allowing a person to forget that this is Alaska's only true urban place. In Fairbanks, the scale is more accommodating. The Tanana Hills are low and round, the high white peaks of the Alaska Range are a distant prospect, a promise. In all these places, it is common for moose to wander on town streets, for foxes and lynx to live on college campuses or behind apartment complexes, for owls or eagles to poach a pet cat, for the occasional wandering bear to pillage a Dumpster site until he has to be dispatched. Great Nature is right outside the door, demanding to be let in.

Color and shape and mountains, rivers, broad valleys, salmon and moose. How do you respond to this world that so insists on being recognized? Accounted for? At minus forty, the world is palpably real.

Writer Donald Barthelme has said that art is a true account of the activity of the mind. For Kes Woodward, the result of coming to Alaska was to throw his mind open to all he saw before him. To try to comprehend it in some artistic fashion. Such comprehension might be thought of as a conversation between an artist and a place, a long and many-faceted conversation. Kes, being Kes, would expect viewers of his work to partake of that conversation as well, to walk into this country as he has done, expansively, and with great curiosity.

Kes says, "The birch is an image for me of the subarctic North." From a comfortable distance, a stand of birch, often covering a whole hillside, seems straight and tall, black and white. The trees become monolithic, a kind of many-columned temple. All the trees are essentially the same. Yet each is significantly different. It is this tension that compels a certain turn of mind. In his series of paintings and oil pastels featuring a solitary birch trunk (and occasionally a pair of them), Kes has explored this tension. His most recent explorations are *Bold Birch* and the *Bright Birch* series of oil pastels. For nearly twenty years, he has made the tree trunk an extended study of the possible range of color and design available in this single and varied image.

Each birch study flirts with the possibility of a perfect vertical parallel structure but resists its neatness. *Bright Birch #2* has a weeping eye made from a branch torn off the trunk and a projecting stob of another branch less cleanly broken. To the right, bark has begun to peel away. The colors on the trunk shift abruptly from patches of lavender, light yellow, burnt orange, to blue and black. After seeing Kes's birches, it is impossible to cut a piece of firewood without considering the elements of its design. Yet it is necessary to regard each painting as a fictive act. The colors and shapes are Kes's abstract explorations made available in a form—a possibility because the tree itself has offered its own manifold variations to anybody who takes the time to look.

As Kes would put it, the trunk of a birch tree "is abstract yet meaningful to the place." To the outsider imagining it, Alaska is too often all white, a blank canvas waiting to be filled with meaning. But like most of the Alaska landscape below the snow line, birches are rich in color and variety. The tree becomes synecdochic in its ability to represent much of interior Alaska. It becomes a way of telling others of the richness of the place. It becomes a way for the artist to recollect himself in the woods among acres of these trees. The single birch trunk becomes the way Kes lets himself into the Alaska landscape. The variation of color, of shapes within a shape that a birch trunk offers can be infinitely explored. Once Kes has alerted us to this way of seeing, his explorations become our own.

Kes's studio is a long, narrow room with one good wall suitable for hanging a sizable canvas

BRIGHT BIRCH #2, 2000
oil pastel on paper
42 x 30 inches

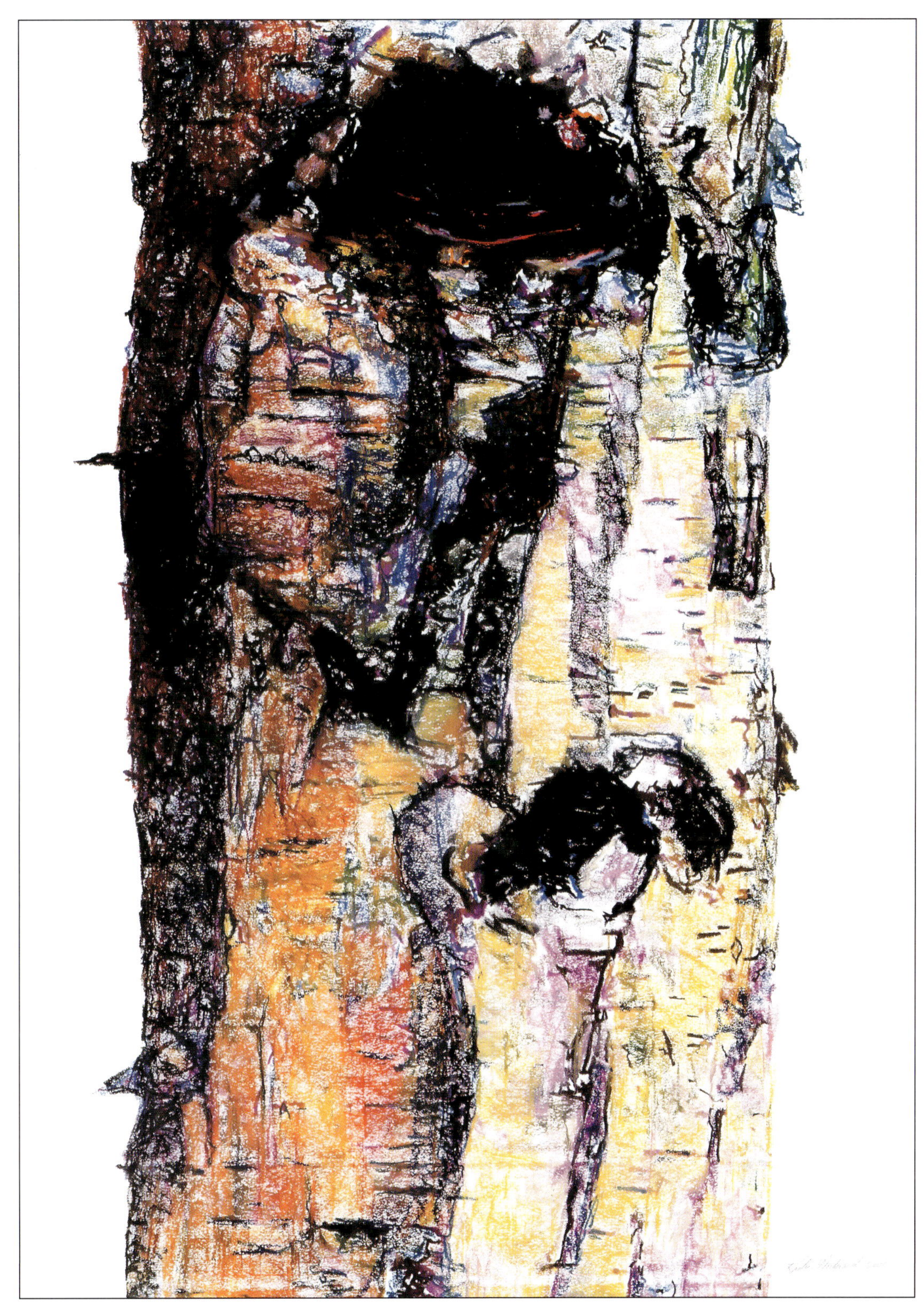

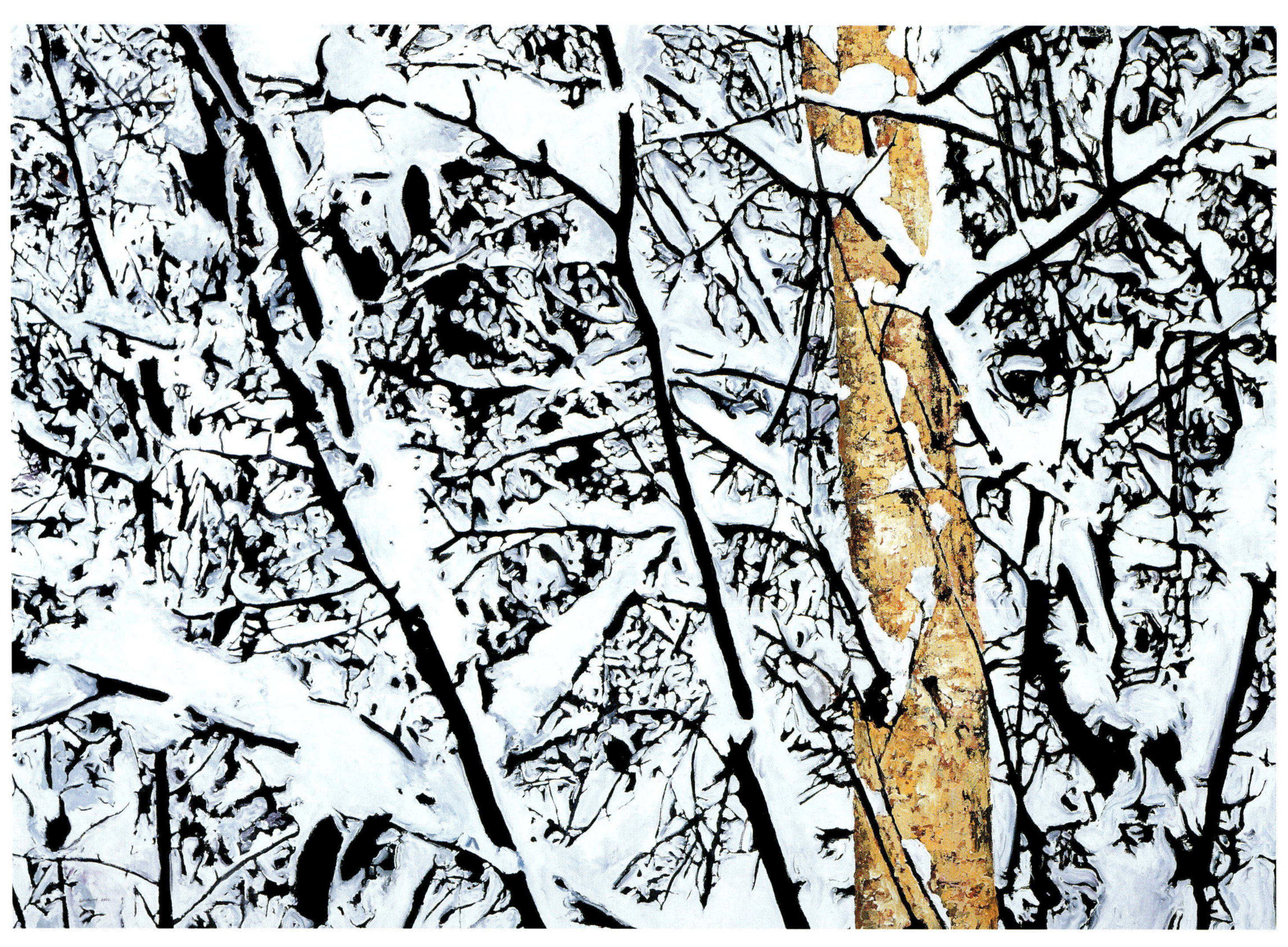

BRIGHT BIRCH, DEEP WINTER, 2000
oil on canvas
59½ x 83½ inches

and working on it in his own particular manner. In working up a painting like *Bright Birch, Deep Winter,* Kes may walk a few miles in that studio, painting an area of a canvas, then walking back to see that area's larger effect. He works close to the canvas with small brushes and paints from the wrist and elbow rather than from the shoulder. When he talks about the actual work of applying paint to canvas, he names his pleasure in sensual and direct terms: "It's fun for me to put paint on in certain ways." One particular way is to paint up to both sides of a line, to explore the interaction of what on first glance might be a series of white panels surrounded by heavy black borders. These are borders described by the dense branches of surrounding trees. Truly, though, there is little purely black here. Within the "black" are explorations of deep green, blue, and brown. These darker colors are suggested by the tint in the white areas made by dragging paint across arbitrary dark/light areas. It's an invitation to look closely. What you see is a constant approaching and falling away from absolute ends of color.

The painting will offer infinite rewards when viewed with your nose barely off the canvas. A step back, and it resolves itself into a near-calligraphic effect, though rougher and more accidental, a style that falls somewhere between Mark Tobey and Robert Motherwell. Finally, though, the long view is of a birch trunk in dense woods, a study in browns surrounded by snow-covered branches. Like many of his wooded Alaska scenes, this one is intentionally cropped. The tops of trees are out of the frame. Viewers feel pressed right up into the woods. There is no familiar path in or out; the painting does not contain the woods, rather they flow out of the frame in all directions. Nature is too unruly to be encompassed here.

The light dry snow and windless conditions in interior Alaska can make the local sparse woods seem impenetrable. Falling snow piles on the skinniest of branches, and it stays in such gravity-defying meringues for days on end. The effect is to flatten perspective; the woods come to be all surface. Kes will tell you that the flattened perspective is a function of the low winter sun. In the long lingering subarctic dawns and twilights, there is just not enough light for our eyes to use to build perspective. The painting's exploration happens on that resulting illusion of surface.

Picture the artist in his narrow studio, walking a worn path between his spot right in front of the canvas to another spot about five paces back. At one end of the path are the questions of color and shape, the questions of the abstract expressionists and color field painters; at the other end are the questions of the representational artist, the questions of the natural world.

I think Kes would tell you that the questions the natural world asks of a painter in Alaska are hard ones. When Sydney Laurence came into this country in the early decades of the twentieth century, he brought his paints and his craft. The Alaska landscape gave him something to paint about. His views of Denali (Mount McKinley) are bathed in pastel light while dense, impenetrable forests and wild rivers push into the foreground. You can't get there, to that lofty summit, from here. The mountaintop is for our aspirations, not our reach: in Laurence's paintings, Alaska becomes the last outpost of the sublime.

Yet for every painter like Laurence, who found his subject in wild rivers and snow-capped peaks, there is somebody like WPA artist Karl Kortess, who stuck to painting the small towns along the Alaska coast because he could find no painterly way to account for the power of the land before him.

Kes Woodward makes a more subdued entry into the Alaska landscape despite all of its insistent clamor. Some of his smaller paintings represent his attention to the Alaska available right nearby, such as a view of the Chena River, or the willow and alder stand on the far bank behind the artist's house. What is striking about his small pieces is the treatment of light and dark, the high skies and their reflection in the river water contrasted to the darker bands of trees and riverbanks. The abstract elements dominate. Setting the horizon line low and darkening the land features allows Kes to work these larger fields for their variation and to de-emphasize the depth of the landscape.

The refusal to let the landscape be simply a landscape has been a distinct feature of most of Kes Woodward's Alaskan painting. The birch trunk paintings isolate a single tree from the forest. And *Bright Birch, Deep Winter* is typical of many winter scenes Kes has depicted in both its resistance to depth and lack of horizon. These methods have enabled the artist to maintain a tension between representation and abstraction. They have also allowed him to make a painterly place for himself where he could work, independent of the extreme demands of the geography. By resisting the more popular view, he has been able to respond directly to that geography without letting it interfere with the development of his own style.

Here's another thing Kes says: "When I move to a new place, I'm often a little bit bewildered." Bewilderment in the literal sense of the word is an expected reaction in Alaska's still mostly pathless terrain. Hikers become bewildered around here all the time. Yet this is the word Kes uses to describe his struggle to find his painterly way into the Southern landscape. It's at these moments that Kes may work with oil pastels, a medium he prefers for his first explorations into an artistic problem. It's at these moments that he might go out and walk the land, do some sketches, and take some photographs. At such moments he may just have to wait, yet I would guess such waiting is an imperative digging at the question using both the front and back of his mind.

Annie Dillard has said, "Young children have no sense of wonder. They bewilder well, but few things can surprise them." Wonder is a sense we acquire as we age, a sense built of comparisons and contrasts. For this reason, it's possible that the country we know best excites no sense of wonderment. We know the land we've walked, its farm roads and cow paths; we know that ridge line, have walked to the top of it and know what's on the other side, too. There is a comfort in knowing a place well.

Yet art is most often a response to the discordant, the unfamiliar; it grows out of a need for reconciliation. In returning to the South, it may have been necessary for Kes to stand farther back in order to see. This longer focal length creates new questions for the painter, new questions of representation. *Appalachian Spring* is a good answer to some of those questions. Here is a deep Virginia wood, like an Alaska wood in the sense that trees are cropped and the dark trunks and branches create a similar abstract exploration of light and dark. What's different is the presence of a horizon line as you'd see it walking toward a ridge top, and the strong white light perhaps coming from a sky of high thin clouds. The understory is brightly lit and, in typical Kes Woodward fashion, more colorful the more it's examined. But the strong backlighting darkens all the trees considerably. The woods-as-surface painting question is now changed to a woods-as-depth question. The Alaska pieces hold a viewer on the edge of a wood. These Southern pieces suggest we are in the woods looking to get out.

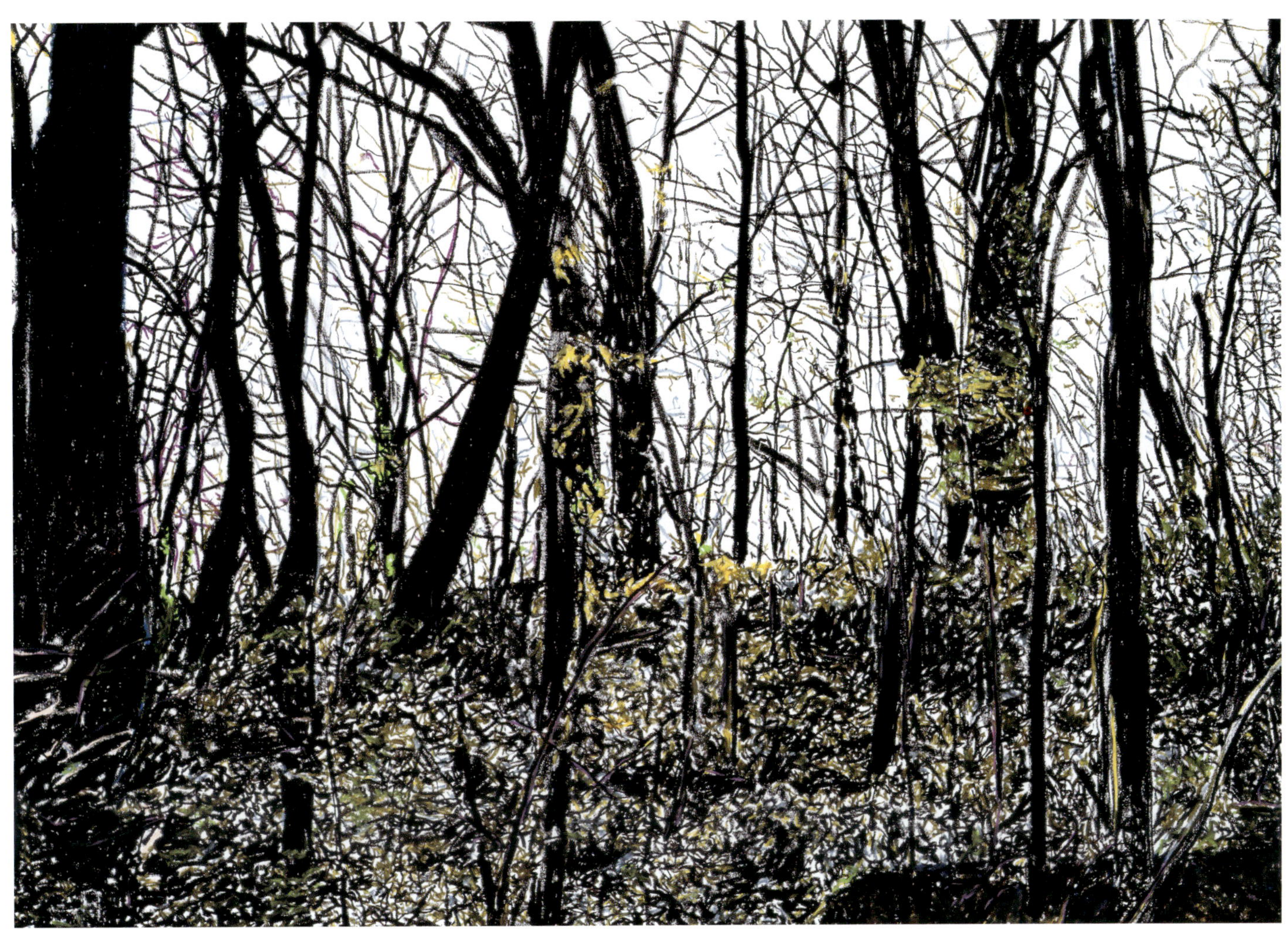

APPALACHIAN SPRING, 2000
oil pastel on paper
30 x 42 inches

Presented with a sinister view of the woods, the Western mind comes to an expected conclusion: Cut them down. Robert Pogue Harrison, in his book, *Forests*, offers a variety of reasons why Westerners fear and resent the woods, but the effect is the same. We cut them down. This stand of trees is clearly not old growth and may even be third- or fourth-growth. Here are young deciduous trees working toward making a high canopy. Yet there is a scrawny but tough understory of trees such as ironwood, dogwood, sourwood, an understory that will remain in place if these woods are allowed to mature. In *Boundary Ridge* we see a more mature wood with bigger trees dominating the foreground and where bright sun makes hard sharp shadows. Even on such a sunny day, the sinister effect of the woods remains.

For people who know the country, these wooded views are full of evidence of human habitation and our effect on the landscape. In Kes's other Southern landscapes, the effect is more straightforward: roads, orchards, fences, and abandoned chimneys regularly form part of the composition. The Alaska landscape rarely admits to a human presence. To be sure, there is much less of a presence here. Most likely, a look into the woods reveals only woods. It's not that Kes has wanted to obscure the fact that he came up on such scenes by roads or trails, but that the immediacy of the image, a single tree, dense stands of woods, doesn't require open space. When admitting to these human-made features, the Southern paintings also acknowledge one of their important effects: an opening out of space, a long view of the land.

Boundary Marker has many of the qualities of a good color field painting. The dense stand of matted grass crossed by the shadows of the old apple trees is a wonderful study of the patterned interplay of greens and blues, a pattern that shifts as the grass gives over to small bushes that climb the bank toward the roadbed. The trunks and branches of the trees have densely constructed color fields as well. Here is one of the long-standing explorations in Kes's work seen yet again. But to step away from this color field is now to see something different: a very deep perspective. Above the orchard is a view of a low distant hill. The scene is inviting; that road could take us anywhere.

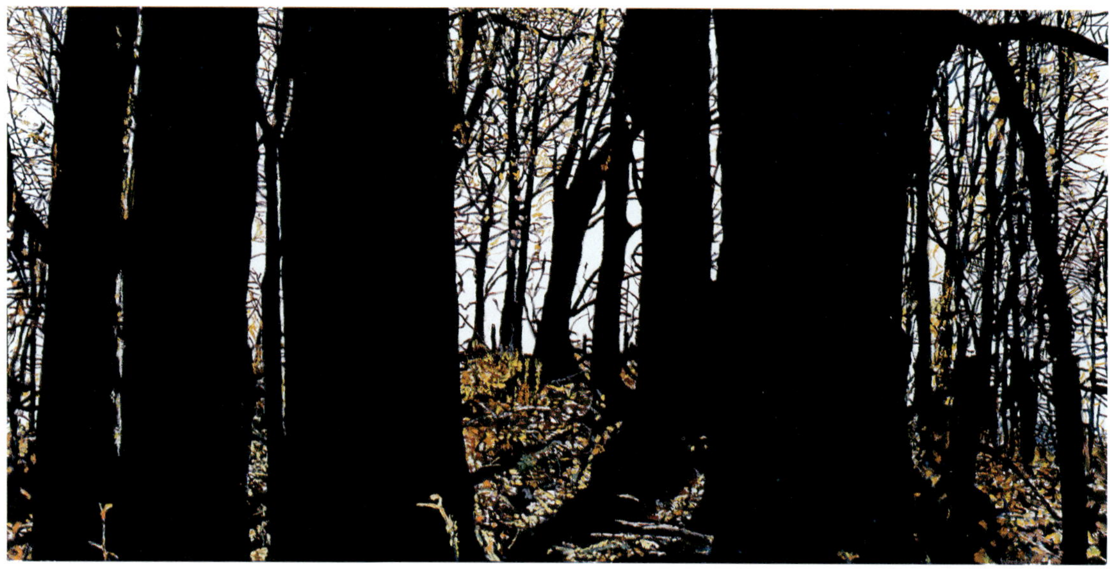

Boundary Ridge, 2000
oil on canvas
29 1/2 x 59 1/2 inches

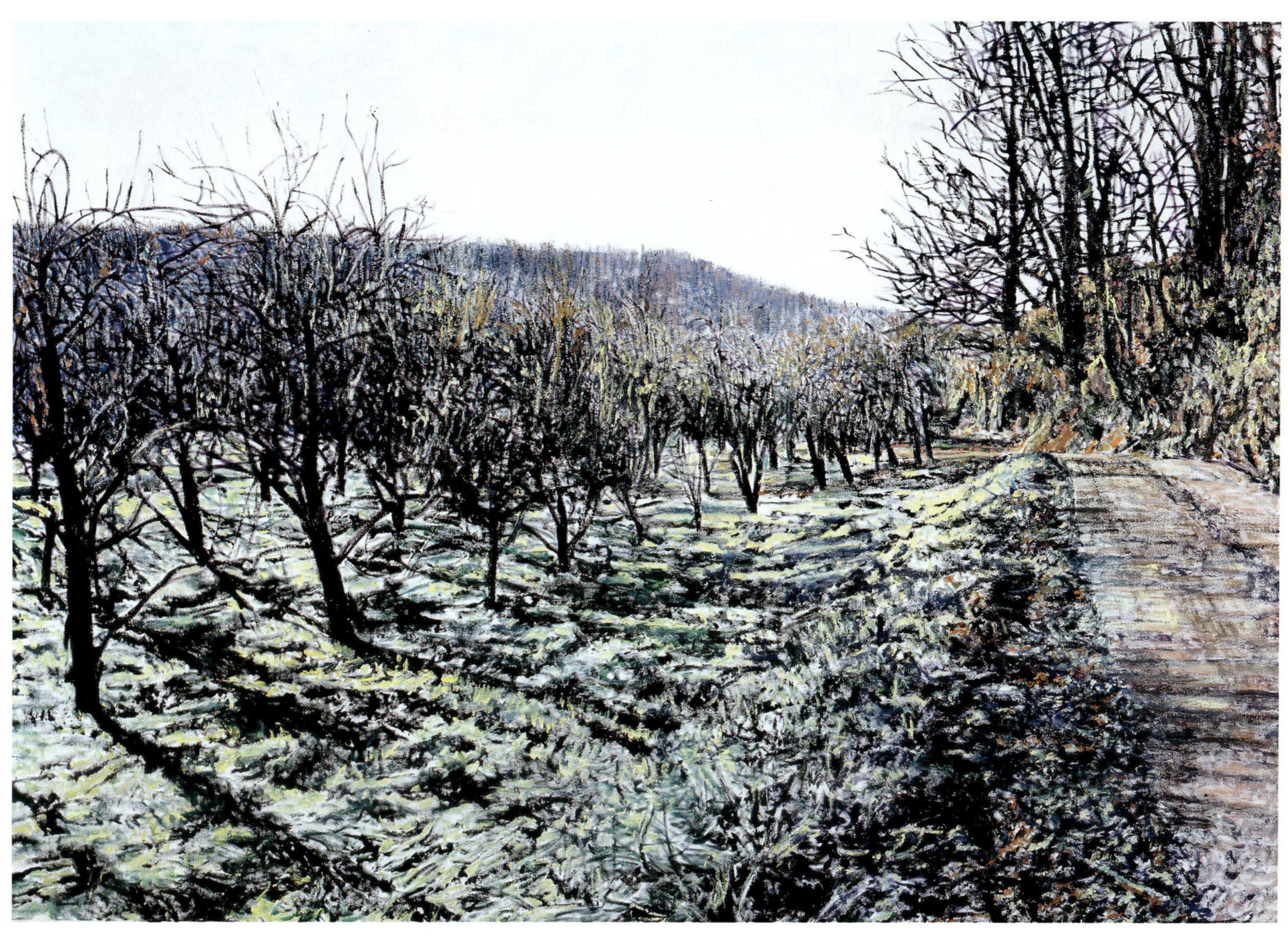

BOUNDARY MARKER, 2000
oil on canvas
59½ x 83½ inches

Of depicting the land, Kes says, "It all has to do with longing." Longing in what way? In the way Odysseus felt longing, perhaps. His was a longing for the far away that open roads in landscapes often allude to. Yet before he was done, he felt the subsequent longing for the familiar, once near at hand, that comes over us as we grow weary of too much strangeness. *At Papa's Cabin* might be the most candidly nostalgic piece in this exhibition. By this artist's standards, it is a rather tame landscape; a pond in the foreground leads up a low draw into mixed woods

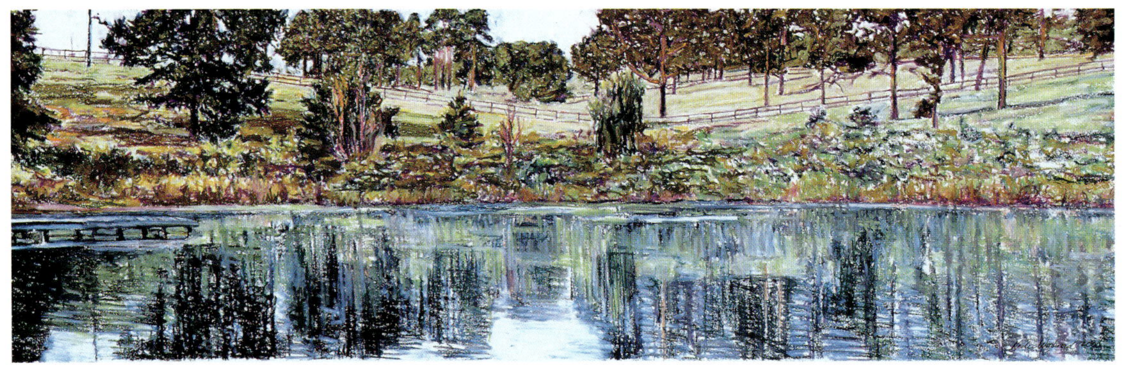

At Papa's Cabin, 2000
oil crayon on paper
12 ¾ x 39 ½ inches

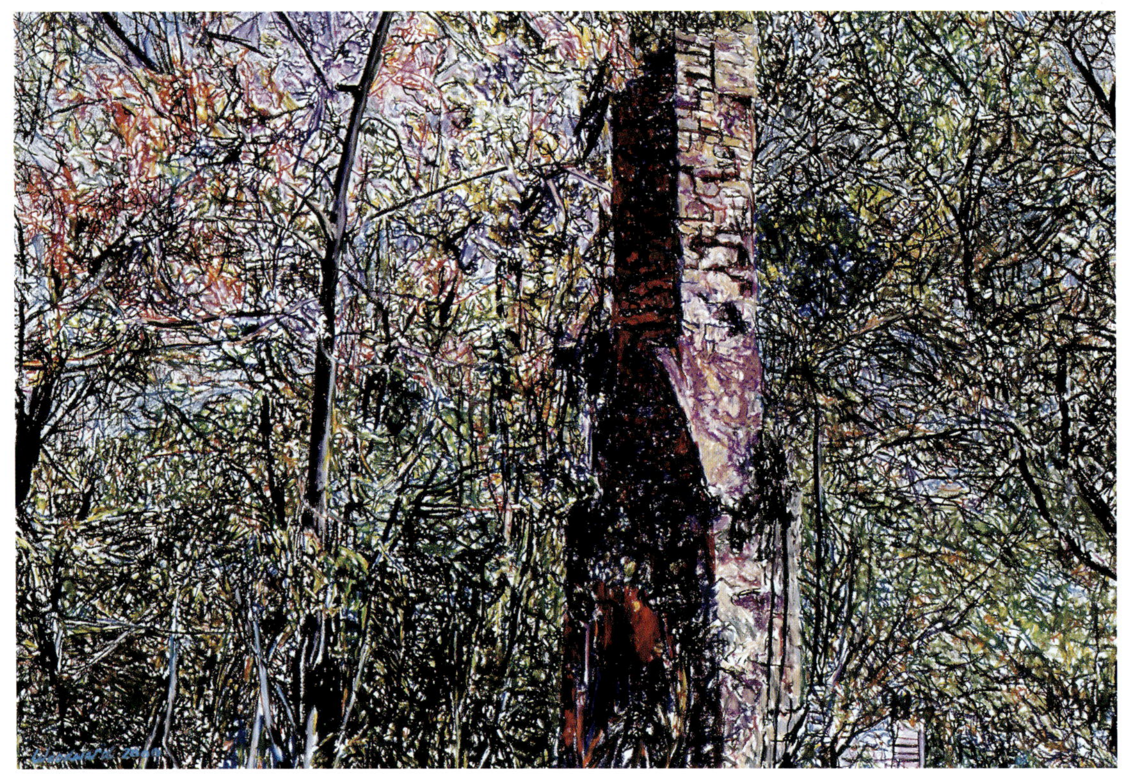

Uncle Phil's, 2000
oil pastel on paper
27½ x 39⅝ inches

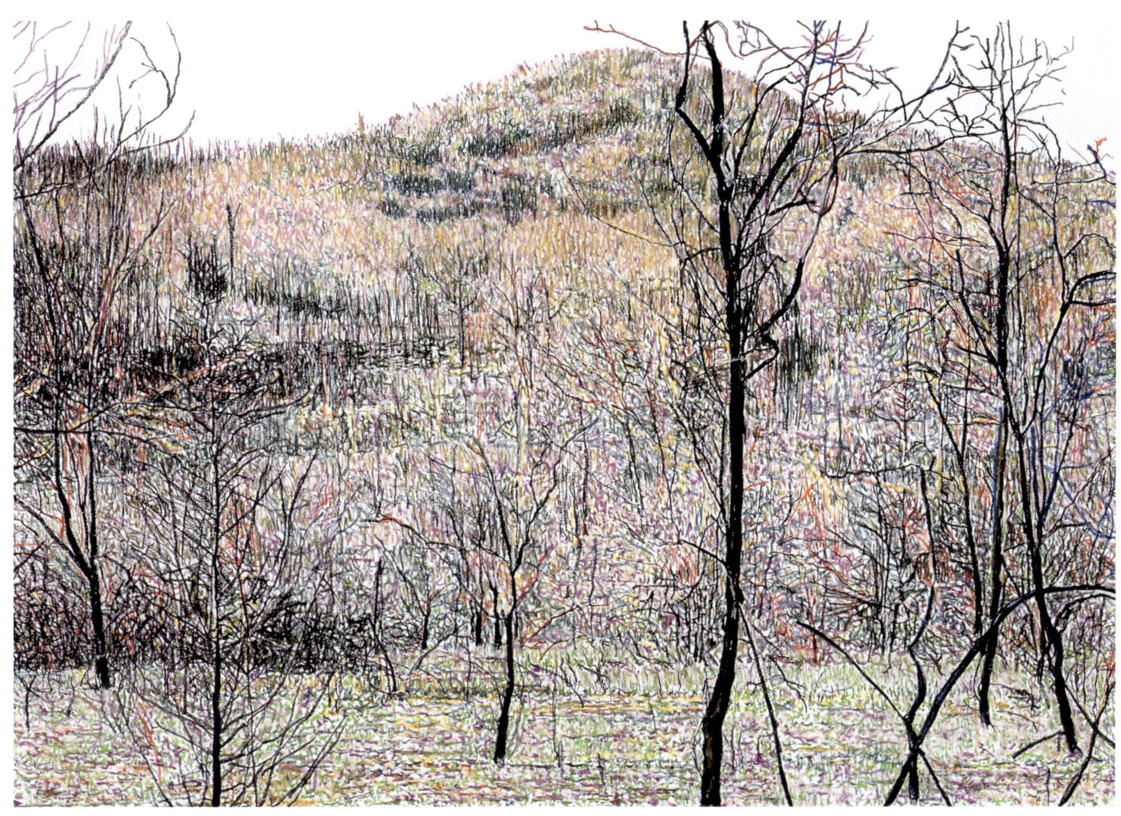

Boaz Mountain Spring, 2000
oil pastel on paper
30 x 42 inches

and pasture. This is his grandfather's old place, a place of family gatherings, a place where Kes can remember catching bluegill and bass from the pond. As a boy he fantasized living in the unseen cabin where we must imaginatively stand to share this view. It could be that the longing Kes describes is that element in art which combines the memory of an actual place with the desires we assign to it. This is the fictive element of landscape, the point at which it moves toward dreamscape.

Of course, the actual and the wishes we might impose on it are most often irreconcilable. Kes's grandfather's land, where he used to run cows, is out of the family. The land itself is just as stubborn in thwarting our desires. What became of the rest of *Uncle Phil's* house? Even the chimney is being worn away. Between weather and conniving animals and plants, Great Nature will tumble it down. But the remains of the old house will not be totally erased from the land.

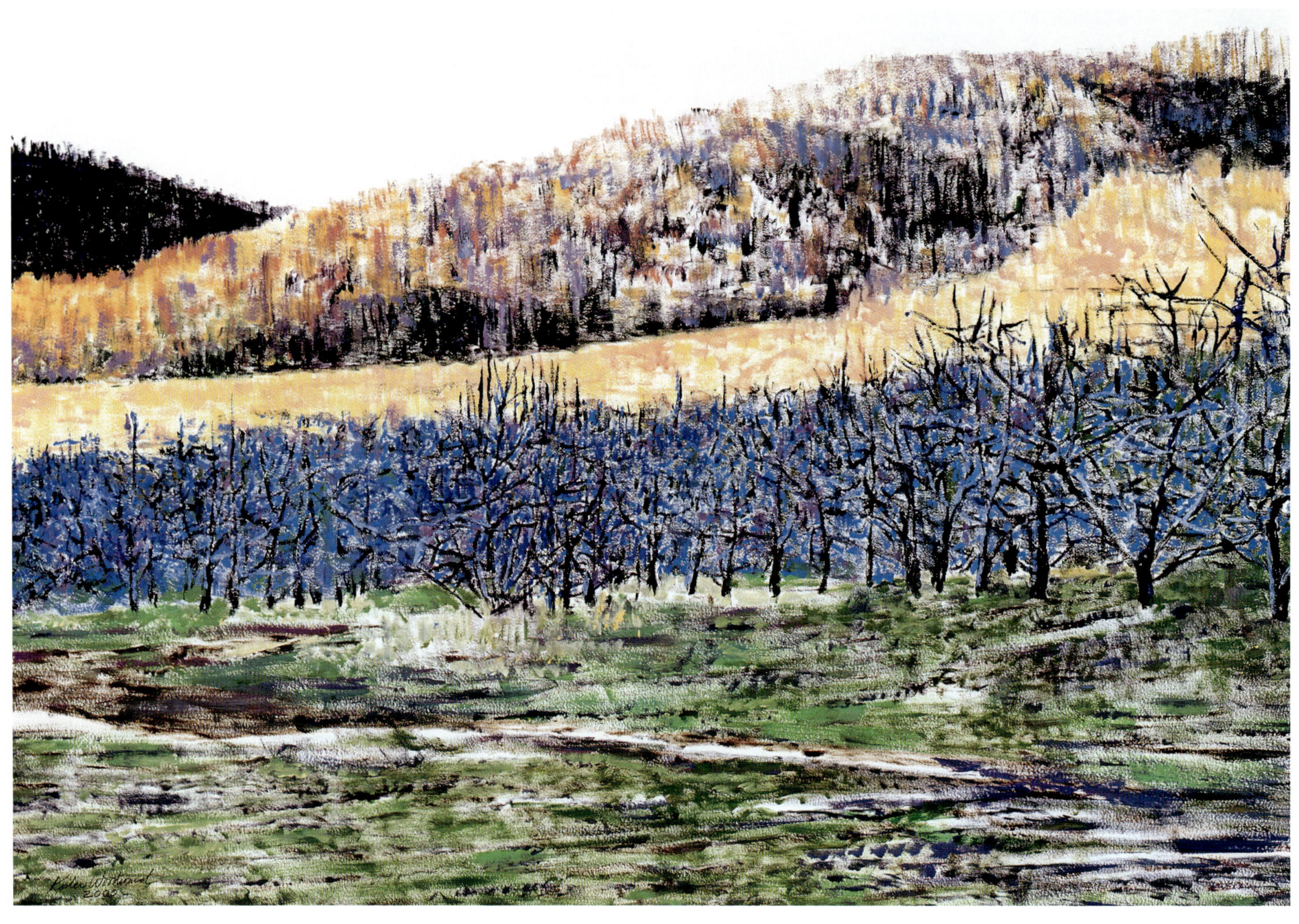

NOVEMBER MORNING, 2000
oil pastel on paper
30 x 42 inches

Many of Kes's Southern pieces seem to be meditations on the tension between our human intentions and what nature might prefer. The apple orchard imposes an order on the land, yet these apple trees seem given over, left to go back to a wilder woods. The human-imposed grid remains; the substory is altered, making an inviting home for deer, more deer today than ever lived east of the Blue Ridge. Vegetation pokes into roadbeds, suggesting that nature will take them back as soon as we stop using them. Yet such abandoned roads remain discernibly worn into the ground long after anybody has walked or driven on them.

Such a human tension with the natural world exists in these Southern paintings in part because the long open spaces offer a chance to see so many more features of the land than Kes's closeups of Alaska woods. How to handle all this open space becomes one of the questions the artist must solve in painting the Southern landscape. *Boaz Mountain Spring* stands as a good solution. The still bare trees in the foreground suggest how early it is in the season. The trees that mount the hill, though, show a range of color, possibly the color that is always present in the smaller limbs of bare trees and possibly that of the leaf buds ready to burst open. The variations within this mass of color lead the eye up the hill. Yet the expansiveness of the space, the sense of open air between the foreground where woods seem to be giving over to pasture to the very top of the hill, pulls the eye as well. There is a long way and a short way to get up that hill. This suggestive power is echoed in *November Morning,* in which a long open field leads to a gradual hillside climb while the eye is also drawn across a wide gap toward the nearly black hill deep in the background.

Kes's use of the available light creates the sense of openness in these Southern pieces. In both early spring and November, the Southern light has a discernible slant. But compared to the extreme slant of light in an Alaskan winter, there remains a wealth of direct available light. This light opens even a wintry landscape; the color makes itself available from a greater distance. You could see into these woods if only you were closer.

Somebody from Alaska might see an irony in going down to the hills and mountains of Virginia and the rolling country of South Carolina and coming upon vistas. Hill folks have always snugged up in the hollows, taking comfort and shelter in the closeness of such places. The Piedmont is an open, welcoming land, but not as compelling to the eye as the mountains. Alaska, though, can offer some valleys tens of miles across and air clear enough to see clean over yonder. Such long views are the very ones that, for twenty-five years in Alaska, Kes has chosen not to represent.

New Mountain, Alaska Range, and *Denali Park September* all come from the variety of views available to those who drive the eastern-most end of the Denali Park Road. By Appalachian standards, these are some kind of mountains, but by Alaska standards, they are smallish peaks. Yet the rockfaces look formidable enough; these are not mountains you might readily walk right up to and over. The long foregrounds in each do, however, suggest that these mountains are approachable, available. Such an approach would be measured in miles, not yards. And anybody who has hiked just a little bit in Denali Park will tell you that the mostly treeless high valley leading to the base of the mountains is tussocky tundra full of low brush and bogs and traveled comfortably only by moose and caribou. Still, if these distant mountains are not physically within easy reach, they have been made to seem within our imaginative reach.

Much of what we are to reach for is contained in the space opened into the landscape by the chosen viewpoint. We stand away and above, a position that suggests a more nearly equal relationship between humans and Great Nature. *Alaska Range,* with its mountaintop that gets

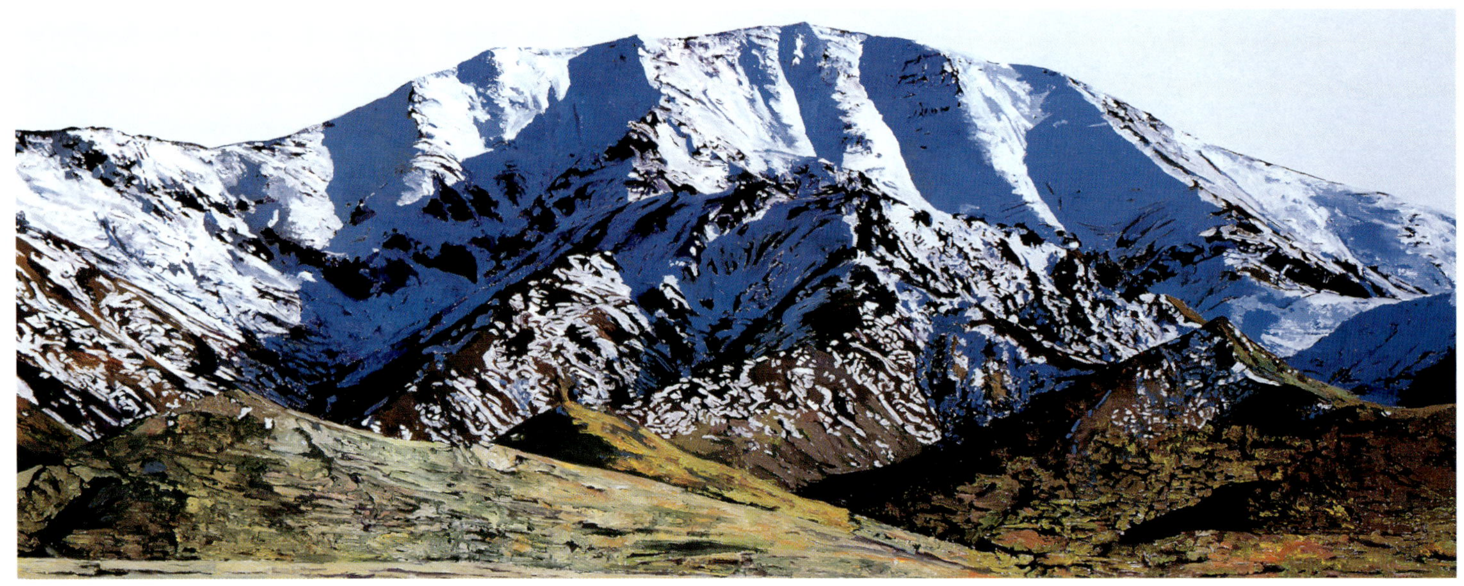

DENALI PARK SEPTEMBER, 2000
oil on canvas
35¹/₂ x 89 inches

away off the top of the canvas, is maybe the best indicator of where our eyes should play: in and around the open colorful space between the mountains and ourselves. Unlike Laurence's foreboding scenes, this perspective makes viewers feel much more a part of the place.

Kes's work has always dwelled in possibility. His first birch paintings were three small panels he did for his wife Missy to welcome her home from a trip. At the time, they were living in downtown Anchorage in a small house set in a birch grove. He found the needed images right outside the window to get him going, and he called that painting *I Like the Birch Trees Best of All.* It's hard to like the sublime; it's akin to liking Jehovah. You just have to stand back before a great roaring sound. Maybe I'm talking about awe here. It's possible to feel considerable awe toward Alaska Range mountains. But the awe-filled person must stand at a respectful distance from the object of awe.

Kes Woodward, it seems to me, has never wanted that of his work. Starting from looking at the birch trees out his window, Kes has let himself enter more deeply into the woods. For those willing to put by the simple question of referential subject matter, abstract painting has always offered its viewers a contract of participation. We stand beside the painter no matter how monumental the canvas may be and help him think it through. When we take such a painting home with us, we get to think it through virtually every day. As he has moved into the representation of the natural world, Kes's work has carried that assumed relationship along with it. A person really can get up every morning and look at one of Kes's birch trunk paintings and think it through in a new and different way.

That participation becomes the shared goal of the landscapes, including those with longer focal lengths than any work Kes has done before. Within each of them are strong elements of color field painting. In addition, there are new elements, new questions about the relationship of land masses and space, a probing of the fictional depth of the canvas.

It is always exciting to see an artist or writer bite off a new piece of the problem he spends his life gnawing at. I think it's fair to say that in being asked to return to the South to paint, Kes found himself looking at the familiar-made-strange as he tried to find his way into that place as a painter. Surprisingly, even to him, these Southern paintings forced some new strategies out of him, some that proved to be useful in Alaska, too.

I have to wonder: down that Denali Park Road is the mountain itself. Will Kes eventually have to take it up? Will he find a way to make it compelling and familiar, disarm it as an icon and return it to us full of fresh wonder? Because that's the sort of thing he's good at.

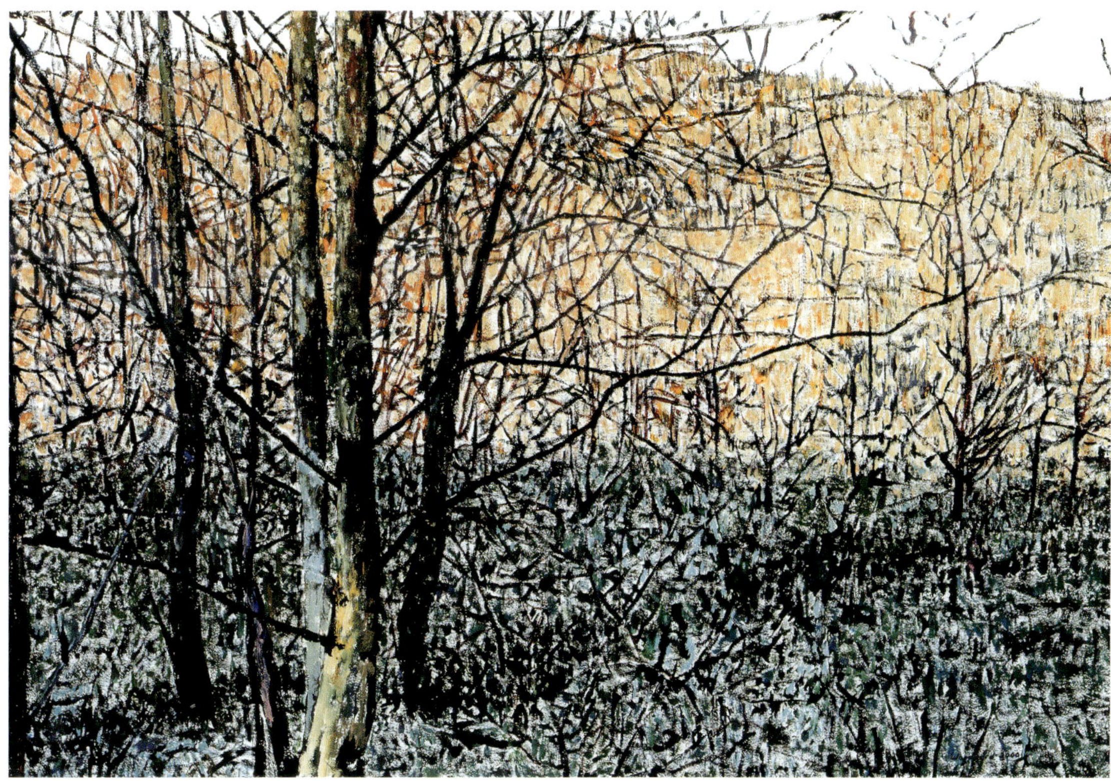

JOHN'S MOUNTAIN, 2000
oil pastel on paper
30 x 42 inches

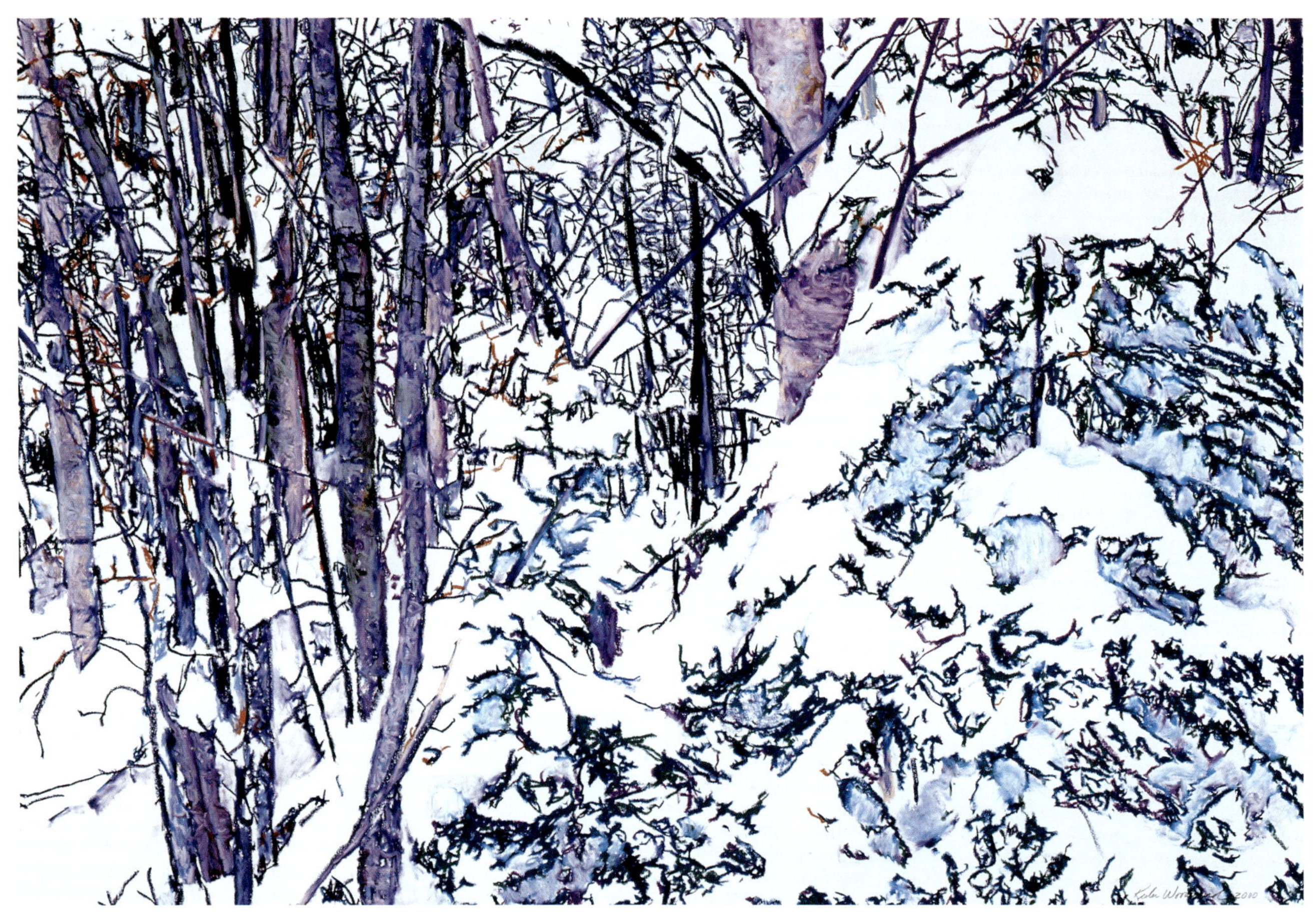

WINTER LIGHT, 2000
oil pastel on paper
27½ x 39½ inches

Kesler E. Woodward

BORN

Aiken, South Carolina, 1951

EDUCATION

- M.F.A., Idaho State University, Pocatello, Idaho, 1977
- B.A., Davidson College, Davidson, North Carolina, 1973

SELECTED AWARDS AND HONORS

- Harriman Scholar and Expedition Artist for *The 1899 Harriman Expedition Retraced*, summer 2001, Smith College and Clark Science Center, Northampton, Massachusetts, 1999
- Emil Usibelli Distinguished Service Award, University of Alaska Fairbanks, 1997
- Museum Recognition Award, University of Alaska Fairbanks Museum, 1994
- External Research Associate, Institute for Arctic Studies, Dartmouth College, Hanover, New Hampshire, 1994-present
- Visiting Research Fellow, Institute on Canada and the United States, Dartmouth College, Hanover, New Hampshire, 1989-1991
- Artist-in-Residence, Anchorage Historical and Fine Arts Museum, Anchorage, Alaska,1982
- Individual Artist Fellowship, Alaska State Council on the Arts, 1981

TEACHING EXPERIENCE

- Professor of Art Emeritus, University of Alaska Fairbanks, 2000-present
- Professor, painting, University of Alaska Fairbanks, 1996-2000
- Associate Professor, painting, University of Alaska Fairbanks, 1988-1995
- Assistant Professor, painting and design, University of Alaska Fairbanks, 1982-1988

SELECTED SOLO EXHIBITIONS

- Morris Museum of Art, Augusta, Georgia, 2001
- Jerald Melberg Gallery, Charlotte, North Carolina, 2001, 1997, 1993, 1990, 1988, 1986, 1985
- Decker-Morris Gallery, Anchorage, Alaska, 1999
- New Horizons Gallery, Fairbanks, Alaska, 1999
- Stonington Gallery, Anchorage, Alaska, 1992, 1988, 1986, 1985, 1984
- Anderson Art Center, Anderson, South Carolina, 1994
- Site 250 Gallery, Fairbanks, Alaska, 1996, 1994
- Alaska Pacific University, Anchorage, 1994
- Anchorage Museum of History and Art, Anchorage, Alaska, 1991, 1983
- University of Alaska, Anchorage, 1991
- University of Alabama, Huntsville, 1990
- Marianne Partlow Gallery, Olympia, Washington, 1988
- Lavender Grey Gallery, Juneau, Alaska, 1982
- The Gathering, Ketchikan, Alaska, 1981
- Civic Center Gallery, Fairbanks, Alaska, 1981
- John B. Davis Art Gallery, Idaho State University, Pocatello, 1977

SELECTED GROUP EXHIBITIONS

- Jerald Melberg Gallery, Charlotte, North Carolina, annually since 1987
- Jerald Melberg Gallery, Charleston, South Carolina, 1999, 1998
- Works on Paper, New York, New York, 1999
- Miami Art Expo, Miami, Florida, 1999
- *Frontier Sublime,* Morris Museum of Art, Augusta, Georgia, 1997
- *Big Paintings,* New Horizons Gallery, Fairbanks, Alaska, 1997
- *Miniatures,* New Horizons Gallery, Fairbanks, Alaska, annually since 1994
- *True North,* Anchorage Museum of History and Art, Anchorage, Alaska, 1996
- *25th Anniversary Exhibition,* Anchorage Museum of History and Art, Anchorage, Alaska, 1993

- *Contemporary Work from Alaska,* Magadan Civic Gallery, Magadan, Russia, 1992
- Denver National Print Fair, Denver, Colorado, 1992
- *South Carolina Artists,* Greenville County Museum of Art, Greenville, South Carolina, 1991
- South Carolina State Museum, Columbia, South Carolina, 1989
- DeRoux-Terzis Gallery, Juneau, Alaska, 1988
- Lawrence Gallery, Portland, Oregon, 1988
- The White House, Washington, D.C., 1988
- Michel Gallery, Seattle, Washington, 1986
- Stonington Gallery, Anchorage, Alaska, 1986, 1985
- University of Alaska Museum, Fairbanks, 1984, 1983
- Lavender Grey Gallery, Juneau, Alaska, 1983
- Cheney-Cowles Museum, Spokane, Washington, 1982
- United States Art in Embassies Program, Brasilia, Brazil, 1982
- University of South Carolina Aiken, 1974
- Gallery of Contemporary Art, Winston-Salem, North Carolina, 1973

SELECTED COLLECTIONS

- Alaska Airlines Corporate Collection
- Alaska Contemporary Art Bank
- Alaska Marine Highway System
- Alaska State Museum, Juneau
- Anchorage Museum of History and Art, Anchorage, Alaska
- The Athletic Club, Charlotte, North Carolina
- Atlantic Richfield Company Corporate Collection
- British Petroleum Corporation Alaska, Anchorage, Alaska
- The Cato Corporation, Charlotte, North Carolina
- Davidson College, Davidson, North Carolina
- Deloitte & Touche, LLP, Charlotte, North Carolina
- Denali Center, Fairbanks, Alaska
- Federal Reserve Bank of Richmond, Charlotte, North Carolina
- Guest Quarters Hotel, Charlotte, North Carolina
- Hunton & Williams, Charlotte, North Carolina
- Idaho State University, Pocatello, Idaho

- Juneau Empire Collection, Juneau, Alaska
- KPMG Peat Marwich & Co., Charlotte, North Carolina
- Morris Communications Corporation, Augusta, Georgia
- NationsBank, Charlotte, North Carolina
- Olympia Community Hospital, Olympia, Washington
- Piedmont Bank & Trust, Davidson, North Carolina
- Price Waterhouse, Charlotte, North Carolina
- Spectrum Properties, Charlotte, North Carolina
- Spaulding & Slye Corporation, Charlotte, North Carolina
- Tacoma Art Museum, Tacoma, Washington
- Tower Club, Charlotte, North Carolina
- Transamerica Reinsurance Corporation, Charlotte, North Carolina
- Tryon Equities, Charlotte, North Carolina
- University of Alaska Museum, Fairbanks
- Westin Hotel, Charlotte, North Carolina
- Xerox Corporation

SELECTED PUBLICATIONS BY KESLER WOODWARD

- Ed., with Frank Soos. *Under Northern Lights: Writers and Artists View the Alaskan Landscape.* Seattle: University of Washington Press, 2000.
- "Painting Alaska." *Alaska Geographic,* vol. 27, no. 3 (September 2000).
- *Spirit of the North: The Art of Eustace Paul Ziegler.* Augusta, Georgia: Morris Communications Corporation in association with the Anchorage Museum of History and Art and the Morris Museum of Art, 1998.
- *A Sense of Wonder.* Fairbanks, Alaska: University of Alaska Museum, 1995.
- *Painting in the North: Alaskan Art in the Anchorage Museum of History and Art.* Anchorage: Anchorage Museum of History and Art; distributed by University of Washington Press, Seattle, 1993.
- *Sydney Laurence, Painter of the North.* Seattle: University of Washington Press in association with Anchorage Museum of History and Art, 1990.
- *Selection, Reconstruction, and Invention: Paintings and Constructions by Paul Gardinier.* Anchorage, Alaska: Anchorage Museum of History and Art, 1989.

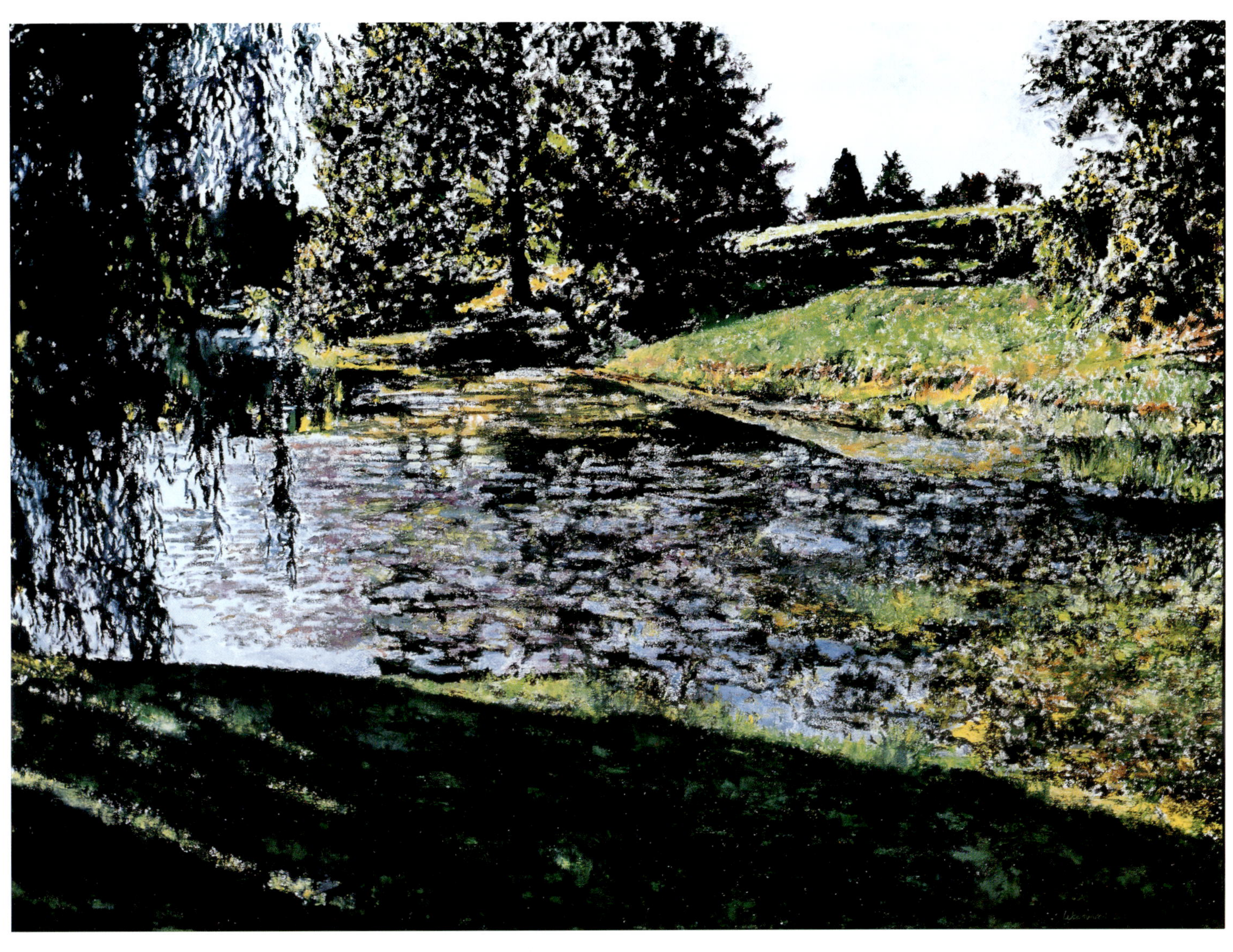

POND SHADOWS, 2000
oil/alkyd on canvas
35¹/₂ x 47¹/₂ inches

SELECTED BIBLIOGRAPHY:
BOOKS AND EXHIBITION CATALOGUES

- Decker, Julie. *Icebreakers: Alaska's Most Innovative Artists.* Anchorage, Alaska: distributed in the United States by Decker Art Services, 1999.
- Driscoll, John. *The Artist and the American Landscape.* Cobb, California: First Glance Books, 1998.
- Jonaitis, Aldona, ed. *Looking North: Art from the University of Alaska Museum.* Seattle: University of Washington Press, 1998.
- Pennington, Estill Curtis. *Frontier Sublime: Alaskan Art from the Juneau Empire Collection.* Augusta, Georgia: Morris Museum of Art, 1997.
- Smith, Shaw. *Kesler Woodward: The Endurance of Wonder.* Charlotte, North Carolina: Jerald Melberg Gallery, 1992.
- Soos, Frank. *Kes Woodward: Inscapes and Poethics, the James Bay Paintings.* Anchorage: University of Alaska's Anchorage Art Gallery, 1991.
- ____ *Bamboo Fly Rod Suite: Reflections on Fishing and the Geography of Grace.* Athens: University of Georgia Press, 1999. 20 illustrations and cover art by Kesler Woodward.

RECENT COMMISSIONS

- Federal Public Art Commission. Four large paintings for Elmendorf Pacific Rim Hospital, Eagle River, Alaska, 1997
- Painting for official poster of Alaska-Canada Arctic Winter Games, 1988
- Paintings on Paper for Alaska Governor's Awards in the Arts, 1986.

BOARDS AND PANELS

- Board of Trustees, Western States Arts Federation, 1998-present
- Alaska State Council on the Arts, 1997-present, appointed by Governor Tony Knowles
- Alaska Humanities Forum Speakers Bureau, 1997-1999
- Visual Arts Panelist, Alaska State Council on the Arts, 1991-1994
- Visual Arts Panelist and Organizations Panelist, Vermont Council on the Arts, 1989-1991
- Board of Directors, Western States Arts Foundation, 1987-1988
- Alaska State Council on the Arts, 1986-1988, appointed by Governor Steve Cowper
- Alaska State Council on the Arts, 1983-1986, appointed by Governor Bill Sheffield
- Public Art Advisory Panel, Alaska State Council on the Arts, 1979-1988

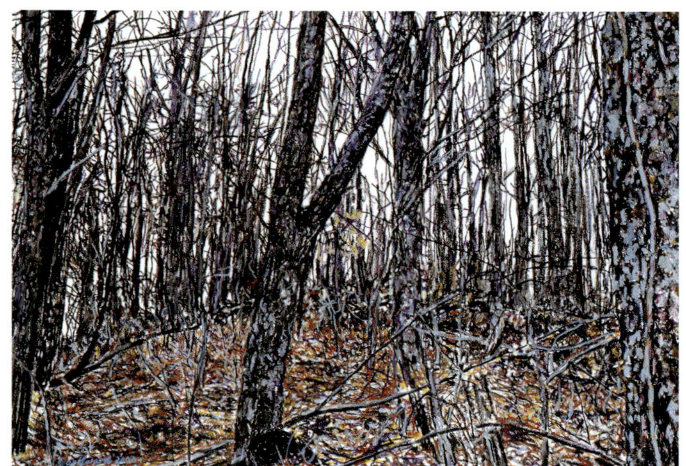

CAROLINA WINTER, 2000
oil pastel on paper
27½ x 39⅝ inches

Index of Illustrations

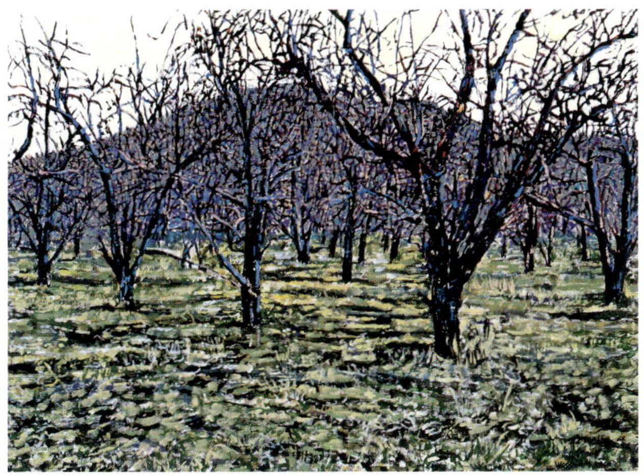

THE ORCHARD IN NOVEMBER, 2000
oil on board
18 x 24 inches

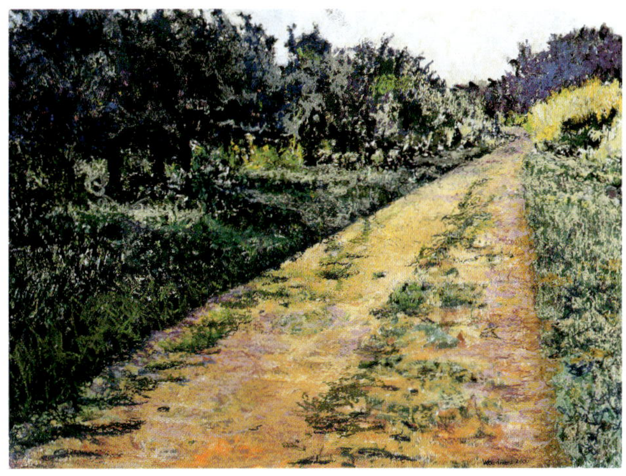

ORCHARD ROAD, 2000
oil crayon on board
18 x 24 inches

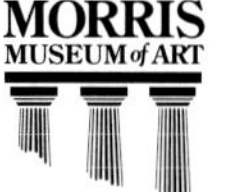
MORRIS
MUSEUM of ART